Dryads and Nymphs

Nicol Maciejewska

BookLeaf
Publishing

India | USA | UK

Presentation by *BookLeaf Publishing*

Web: www.bookleafpub.com

E-mail: info@bookleafpub.com

ISBN: 9789363316751

First edition 2024

To all my lovers--past and present. The swirl of emotions within me seems to arise from our highs and lows. Thank you, but now, I am so much more.

PREFACE

"Dryads and Nymphs" is an anthology that delves into themes of unrequited love, metaphysical influences, and the whimsical world of fashion. Poetry has always been my tool for expressing emotions and discovering their deeper meanings. This release follows my debut poetry collection, "Tell Me Your Dreams," published in 2023.

Midnight Pursuit

I grasp onto this thread that connects us two
My last vestige of memories not yet formed
Will your face still sour at the sight of me and
words of wrath exchanged?
Am I to spend the remainder of my time on this
earthly plane
with an inch of filth upon my skin?
Tainted--with no absolution earned

Your ghost proceeds to haunt me on these
Brooklyn streets
There are hidden messages wherever I gaze, left
behind to mock me
and for me to feel shame
I wonder if you've seen my messages of
remorse.
Or is this yet another hopeless endeavor... just
another midnight pursuit?

A La Chambre

Dripping carbon candlesticks with wicks set
ablaze
Tales from the crypt can be heard amid the
smoking sage
Herbs de Provence and shards of tourmaline
A swinging pendulum with messages from the
divine

Emulsion regurgitation deterioration leaving
behind piercing irises
That look over all just as Dr. T.J. Eckleburg's
eyes did
Memory captured in black and white with scarlet
petals trapped in the frame
Message written by lovers with bleeding ink can
be seen across the page

Artificial sun and painted blood moon light up
the room
Oil on canvas with a noxious odor of mineral
spirits lingering through
Dryads and nymphs frolic within their
brush-stroked lush foliage
Brittle bone and bovine skull neatly lay in indigo

Numbing coldness permeates within the
adolescent cage
Keeping warm with cauldron fire and starry
crochet
Hidden is a world undiscovered until its
occupant meets the grave
There'll be no need to travel far, for tombstones
of the Sacred Heart lie twenty feet away

Romance Languages

Wallpapered rose and peony
Amid dimly lit flames
At Rue de Bons Enfants and Café de Flore
In ancient stone, I find my temporary home
Across the Atlantic, a long way from what I call
my own

America still lingers, singing its tune on the
radio
Moment by moment it becomes drowned out by
the Parisian streets
While I search for a place where I can retreat

Now leaving behind my rustic Italian fantasy
Where I found myself behind a stove cooking
for those who I have adored
As time goes on I find myself blooming as the
flora that climbs the wall
In the dead of Winter, I betray the season and
choose to grow

I migrate now to the Iberian Peninsula to find
warm flesh
Inside blood pumps and fills the chest

Whispers in the wind remind me that I will love
again

Numb

6

We're all lost souls searching for relief
to go one day to the next
and being numbed by love is our best
bet----

A Seance For the Living

Vanish souls--
Untethered from the plane
Leaving oneself without
A singular embrace

Leaving the body in a mesmerized state
Unable to navigate
Hypnotized--entranced--
The doing of one who doesn't give a chance

Sweet adolescent innocence
Turning rotten--sour--
Spoiled by the spirits who whisper death
Summoned by the demons living in your head

Spit out the ectoplasm!
Release yourself from the shadow
Tether to the plane
Live in thy flesh once again

S. Inferno

Hyperrealism exploration within a plane of
limitation
Executed through hours with precise
manipulation
Framed in surrealist fluctuations

The fear of art transmutes into a fear of doubt
that looms within your soul
As we descend further into the dark wood we
wonder if release can be found within these nine
circles
Or are we to suffer forevermore

We seek out bravery from the Himalayas, the
Sahara, the Black Forrest
Avoiding the bitter sins of lust, pride, and
avarice
We look up at the Heavenly Bodies hidden
behind pearlescent gates
They reside inside with chests and toes painted
gold and with masks made of bronze

While the onyx snake constricts my neck
I feel compelled to fulfill her expectations

To release we must risk it all and give in to
divine creation
Only then can we rise out of the Inferno by
following the cosmos to reach Paradiso
And we will remain there by decoupling
ourselves from a fear that we creators hold so
dear

Maybe One Day

Sometimes love isn't enough
Even though I earnestly wanted it to be
I think about it all too often
All the changes that could've been made
If only just one compromise would've helped us
endure
I search for that fatal misstep that left us
tumbling down
Shattering...
Breaking...
All that we've cared for
It pushed us to follow our patterns of blondes
and brunettes
Now all I have left are those recordings
Which play incessantly in my head
like a needle getting caught on a scratched
groove
And I worry that it'll never stop
What if I can't stop loving you
All because our love wasn't enough

Can We Love Again?

Sleepless in the 1st arrondissement
as my thoughts are infested with
this unfulfilled longing

Seemingly feeling as if the
path I've chosen is one I
cannot see through

My truth seems to be that I
belong with you even though
at times I don't want to

But it's you, It's always been you
a soul unable to be replicated
in another vessel

And I wish to control it,
but it's useless for I feel
powerless.

I keep trying to figure out what it
is about you that keeps me entranced
as there are still many aspects of you
that I don't quite understand

If I want you I could confess it all
and be found wrapped in your embrace
and pretend that what was spoken
between us no longer matters
for it does

But here I am

Not sleeping because it is you I desire to
lie next to me again.

Ashes of Admiration

You slip into my dreams while I'm wide awake
Seeing pieces of you where your mark was made
It is all that now remains
I'll save and cherish these ashes of admiration
The residue of our loving hue
The memories are now all that's true

Changes in the season have made changes in the
flesh
What was is now what you detest
The sliver of happiness leaves your face and
mine
A lour is now painted where that smile did once
reside

I'm left with nothing but trinkets
And songs never to be finished
Old promises now linger… never to be fulfilled
But my crippled heart lives on or at least it one
day will

Golden Wings

An angel fell from the heavens and wrapped me
in golden wings
Shielding me from what I no longer dare to see
The light refracts from crystal tears
And on these moonlit nights, I began to see
There was never any truth to those conjured
fantasies
My grief stayed dormant for many moons, but
now I'm unsure I can endure
And I look to see if your pain shines through
But in my visions, I see nothing but the glimmer
of gold

Mist

The strangeness in the haze
Vivid feelings lost in a maze
I try to grasp their meaning
But these ghosts continue retreating
Appearing and disappearing

I search for answers in the world
In its details, they're unfurled
Bit by bit
The mist seems to lift

Forbidden

I sealed my fate with a kiss
and you were the forbidden fruit
begging to get bitten.
Will I feel God's wrath
if I pursue this sinful path?
Are you secretly the devil
coaxing me to do my worst?
Tell me, am I cursed?

Drought

17

You and I are scorched earth and nothing left can
bloom.
Yet we wait for a cloudless rain, hoping our tears
can water the parched soil.

Dream Creep

Another night
Another flight
Into the realm of dreams
bleaker than life
Because I see what could be
Instead of what should be

Chased around
By a foe
Who's charmed me into believing it's right
To dream of a kiss so wrong

Grrrls

The scene contained people who were not mine
The only thing they see is the shape of me
Defined by curves
Obtuse even crossed their minds

Pitting women against women
Thrusting your rock rivalries
Waving the phallic head of your 6-string
Believing your voice is the only one that should
be heard

Clouded by privilege
In the star only you could be reflected
Threatened by triumph
You say, "Women can't do what I can"

Sour tongues sting
Leaving you raw
How can one see the unseen
Know the errors, know the flaws
Your people are not my people

I refuse. I revolt. I riot.

Resilience

I admire my light's resilience
as even in moments of stagnancy
my spark remains unextinguished.

I'm still here in my flesh--
there's no need for the funeral just yet.

Go My Own Way

I can't hear the summer rain
Behind the window pane
I just hear your words
drag on and on and on and on

I can't feel the wind no more
My mind aches and I feel sore
I just hear your words
drag on and on and on and on

Etched in my memory are all the things that I
can't see
Little reminders of everything you were to me
Sleepless nights await me, I can't drift back to
sleep
But what's the point anyway, I'll see you there in
my dreams

Avoiding the places that were once our space
It was time I gave up this endless chase
I'm no longer a pawn in your reckless game
I fear I've been used so it's time to go my own
way

Abysmal Abyss

The poison hasn't left my bloodstream
I still am who I was
Older, but not wiser
I thought I changed for the better
Yet I cling on to the same mistakes that I've
made before
Wasn't I happy?
Oversaturated with choices
Has made me even more indecisive
Now I'm trapped in the abysmal abyss of my
mind
Figuring out what I sho

Out of our control

The smooth winds flow
When all was grand
But what did we know
That ruin would come to all that we had planned

Running wild on mysteries
Stories told long ago
Finding the clue that would somehow restore the
world a new, but alas
Drowning in red herrings is all that's come too

Caught up with distractions
Waiting for the rapturous winds to come to a halt
Hoping consequences come with actions
Finally removing the blindfold
The one that's kept us controlled